How To Use This Study Guide

This five-lesson study guide corresponds to *"What To Teach Your Children"* *With Rick Renner* (Renner TV). Each lesson in this study guide covers a topic that is addressed during the program series, with questions and references supplied to draw you deeper into your own private study of the Scriptures on this subject.

To derive the most benefit from this study guide, consider the following:

First, watch or listen to the program prior to working through the corresponding lesson in this guide. (Programs can also be viewed at **renner.org** by clicking on the Media/Archives links or on our Renner Ministries YouTube channel.)

Second, take the time to look up the scriptures included in each lesson. Prayerfully consider their application to your own life.

Third, use a journal or notebook to make note of your answers to each lesson's Study Questions and Practical Application challenges.

Fourth, invest specific time in prayer and in the Word of God to consult with the Holy Spirit. Write down the scriptures or insights He reveals to you.

Finally, take action! Whatever the Lord tells you to do according to His Word, do it.

For added insights on this subject, it is recommended that you obtain Rick Renner's book *The Point of No Return: Tackling Your Next New Assignment With Courage and Common Sense*. You may also select from Rick's other available resources by placing your order at **renner.org** or by calling 1-800-742-5593.

TOPIC

Teach Your Children To Love Jesus Above All Else

SCRIPTURES

1. **Proverbs 22:6** — Train up a child in the way he should go: and when he is old, he will not depart from it.

SYNOPSIS

The five lessons in this study on *What To Teach Your Children* will focus on the following topics:

- Teach Your Children To Love Jesus Above All Else
- Teach Your Children To Repent
- Teach Your Children To Honor Authority
- Teach Your Children To Work
- Teach Your Children To Value Material Possessions and To Be Thankful

The emphasis of this lesson:

The number one, most important, thing to teach your children — and grandchildren — is to love Jesus above all else.

Today if you visit the archaeological museum in Antakya, Turkey, you will see mosaics of a First Century house near the city of Seleucia. This home and many others like it were around during the very time the apostle Paul launched into his apostolic ministry. They featured majestic columns and ornate frescos and housed real families. Husbands and wives worked to raise their children and prepare them for adulthood. It was to these parents that Paul first wrote and gave instruction on how to train their children.

Rick and Denise Renner have been blessed with three amazing sons — Paul, Philip, and Joel. They are all grown now and have families of their own. In addition to loving Jesus and following Him, each one serves in a

A Note From Rick Renner

I am on a personal quest to see a "revival of the Bible" so people can establish their lives on a firm foundation that will stand strong and endure the test as end-time storm winds begin to intensify.

In order to experience a revival of the Bible in your personal life, it is important to take time each day to read, receive, and apply its truths to your life. James tells us that if we will continue in the perfect law of liberty — refusing to be forgetful hearers, but determined to be doers — we will be blessed in our ways. As you watch or listen to the programs in this series and work through this corresponding study guide, I trust you will search the Scriptures and allow the Holy Spirit to help you hear something new from God's Word that applies specifically to your life. I encourage you to be a doer of the Word He reveals to you. Whatever the cost, I assure you — it will be worth it.

> Thy words were found, and I did eat them;
> and thy word was unto me the joy and rejoicing of mine heart:
> for I am called by thy name, O Lord God of hosts.
> — Jeremiah 15:16

Your brother and friend in Jesus Christ,

Rick Renner

Unless otherwise indicated, all scripture quotations are taken from the *King James Version* of the Bible.

Scripture quotations marked (*AMPC*) are taken from the *Amplified® Bible, Classic Edition*. Copyright © 1954, 1958, 1962, 1964, 1965, 1987 by The Lockman Foundation. Used by permission. **www.Lockman.org**.

Scripture quotations marked (*NIV*) are taken from *Holy Bible, New International Version®, NIV®* Copyright ©1973, 1978, 1984, 2011 by Biblica, Inc.® Used by permission. All rights reserved worldwide.

Scripture quotations marked (*NKJV*) are taken from the *New King James Version®*. Copyright © 1982 by Thomas Nelson. Used by permission. All rights reserved.

Scripture quotations marked (*TLB*) are taken from *The Living Bible* copyright © 1971. Used by permission of Tyndale House Publishers, Inc., Carol Stream, Illinois 60188. All rights reserved.

Scriptures marked as (*GNT*) are taken from the *Good News Translation - Second Edition* © 1992 by American Bible Society. Used by permission.

Scripture quotations taken from the *New American Standard Bible®* (*NASB*) Copyright © 1960, 1962, 1963, 1968, 1971, 1972, 1973, 1975, 1977, 1995 by The Lockman Foundation. Used by permission. **www.Lockman.org**.

What To Teach Your Children

Copyright © 2019 by Rick Renner
1814 W. Tacoma St.
Broken Arrow, OK 74012-1406

Published by Rick Renner Ministries
www.renner.org

ISBN 13: 978-1-6803-1596-7

ISBN 13 eBook: 978-1-6803-1634-6

All rights reserved. No portion of this book may be reproduced or transmitted in any form or by any means — electronic, mechanical, photocopy, recording, scanning, or other — except for brief quotations in critical reviews or articles, without the prior written permission of the Publisher.

certain area of ministry in the church. The relationships they now share among each other are wonderful, but those relationships did not happen by accident. It took time and consistent effort on the part of the parents to train up their children in the ways of God. If we will follow the wisdom of God's Word and invest in our children, we will reap the benefits of healthy relationships.

Start Building a Solid, Christ-Centered Foundation When They're Young

There are many valuable things to teach your children and grandchildren to produce good, responsible adults. The most important thing — by far — is *to teach them to love Jesus above all else*. What you as their parent establish as priority in their lives when they are young will stay with them when they are older. The Bible confirms this truth in Proverbs 22:6, instructing parents to "train up a child in the way he should go: and when he is old, he will not depart from it."

If you make regular church attendance important to your children when they're little, it will be important to them when they are older. Likewise, if you make reading the Bible, praying, giving tithes and offerings, and serving in the church a priority, these practices will very likely be a priority in your children's lives when they are older and living on their own.

When you do what you can do to connect your children in a vibrant, firsthand relationship with God, you're giving them the very best foundation they can have in life. The Scripture says, "...What a person plants, he will harvest. The person who plants selfishness, ignoring the needs of others —*ignoring God!* — harvests a crop of weeds. All he'll have to show for his life is weeds! But the one who plants in response to God, letting God's Spirit do the growth work in him, harvests a crop of real life, eternal life" (Galatians 6:7,8 *MSG*).

Reading illustrated Bible stories with your children from the time they are toddlers through the growing stages of life is one of the most rewarding habits you can develop with them. They will remember the colorful images and the foundational stories throughout their lifetime. In the same way, creating a library of godly entertainment — books, music, and DVDs — filled with God's Word and songs of worship will instill the truth of God deep within their hearts and continue to play in their ears throughout their adult lives.

Every verse of Scripture, every Bible story, every song of praise and worship your children hear will help to hide the Word in their hearts and give the Holy Spirit truth to draw from to teach them throughout their lifetime. Speaking in regard to His Word, God said, "...It shall not return unto me void, but it shall accomplish that which I please, and it shall prosper in the thing whereto I sent it" (Isaiah 55:11). If you consistently plant the Word into the hearts and minds of your children, it will produce a harvest of godliness in every area of their lives and the lives of those they touch.

Create an Environment That Encourages Healthy Spiritual Growth

Sadly, some parents make a huge mistake and say, "Well, I don't want to make my kids go to church or pressure them to believe a certain way. I want them to make their own decisions when they get older regarding spiritual matters." This is a cunning lie fabricated by the enemy, and it is extremely unwise to follow.

Think about it. How would your children respond if after you woke them up each morning you said, "Hey kids, do you want to go to school today?" In virtually every instance, they would say something like, "No, we don't want to go to school today. We want to stay home and sleep in, watch television, play video games, and hang out with our friends."

The truth is, education is a priority. Thus, we *make* our kids go to school; we don't just hope they get educated on their own. We know how vital it is, and therefore, we consistently work to make sure they're in school getting a proper education. In the same way, we need to see how vital it is for our children to develop spiritually. If you want your children to grow up loving the Lord, you need to treat their spiritual development as important as their educational development.

As a parent, it is your job to create an environment conducive to healthy spiritual development and to train up your children in the ways of God. Take them to church regularly. Start reading the Bible to them when they're little, and teach them to read it for themselves once they are able. Have family devotionals that are age-appropriate and relevant to what they are experiencing in their lives. Encourage them to develop their closest friendships with other Christian kids.

Let's face it. Left to themselves, your children are not going to choose to read and study the Bible, go to church, or serve others. On the contrary, they will naturally gravitate toward a self-centered life absent of God. But if you consistently educate your kids in spiritual matters and do your best to connect them in a personal relationship with Jesus, you are setting them up for success in every area of their adult life.

Jesus said, "For what shall it profit a man, if he shall gain the whole world, and lose his own soul?" (Mark 8:36). The most important thing you can teach your children is their need for salvation and how to know and walk in relationship with God. Yes, it is important to ensure they get a good education and receive the training they need to land a good-paying job. But if they don't know the Lord, they are in trouble. You are raising eternal beings, and if they aren't saved when they pass from this earth, they are going to spend eternity in turmoil.

Cultivate an Appetite in Your Kids for the Things of God

There is an interesting truth about the word "train" found in Proverbs 22:6. In the Hebrew language, the word "train" is connected with one's *taste buds*. Specifically, it depicts parents who start their children out early eating healthy foods — such as fruits, vegetables, whole grains, and lean meats. When those children are full-grown, they will return to eating those same nutritious foods.

On the other hand, if parents train their children's taste buds with junk foods and feed them a diet lacking in real nutritional value, their children's appetite when they are adults will continually draw them back to those same nutrient-deprived foods they were conditioned to eat when they were young.

So when God says, "Train up a child in the way he should go: and when he is old, he will not depart from it," (Proverbs 22:6), He is actually saying, "Give your children — and grandchildren — healthy spiritual taste buds at a young age. Give them a healthy appetite for the things of God when they are young, and when they are older, they won't depart from it." What you condition their spiritual taste buds to eat when they are young is what they will continually be drawn back to when they're older.

And remember, as you are walking through the journey of being a mother or father to your children, don't just focus on the front end — the *training*. Some parents have become so absorbed with the task of training that they overlook the promise on the back end — that when their child is old, he or she will not depart from what they've been taught.

Instead of just concentrating on the work, remember to believe and hope for the reward — that your kids will hold on to the instruction you've given them and make it their own as they become adults. There will come a time in the course of your parenting when you have given them all the training they can receive. At that point, your job is to *trust* God's Word and believe it will not return unto Him void — that it will accomplish the very thing He said it would. This is His promise to you.

STUDY QUESTIONS

> Study to shew thyself approved unto God, a workman that needeth
> not to be ashamed, rightly dividing the word of truth.
> — 2 Timothy 2:15

1. Your children's relationship with Jesus is the single most important aspect of their lives. If it is healthy, everything else will fall into place. Take time to meditate on Jesus' words in John 3:16,17; Matthew 22:37,38; and Mark 12:29,30. How do these passages shed new light on God's desire to have a loving relationship with each of your children?

2. Proverbs 22:6 says, "Train up a child in the way he should go: and when he is old, he will not depart from it." In what ways are you seeing the reality of this promise fulfilled in your life? How about in the lives of your older children?

PRACTICAL APPLICATION

> But be ye doers of the word, and not hearers only,
> deceiving your own selves.
> — James 1:22

1. Think back on your own life. In what ways did your parents or grandparents help connect you in a relationship with Jesus? Did they read the Bible to you and pray for you? What can you learn from their example and apply in your own life as a parent?

2. What Bible stories and illustrations can you still remember hearing and seeing when you were a child? How have these stories impacted you through your life?

3. The most important thing you can teach your children is *to love Jesus above all else*. What are you doing to help connect your kids in a

vibrant, personal relationship with the Lord? What new ideas is the Holy Spirit stirring inside you to begin interacting with your children?

TOPIC

Teach Your Children To Repent

SCRIPTURES

1. **Hebrews 12:6** — For whom the Lord loveth he chasteneth, and scourgeth every son whom he receiveth.

SYNOPSIS

The ancient city of Antioch was the third largest in the Roman Empire. It was the place where believers were first called Christians. The region all around Antioch was filled with many beautiful homes and villas of all kinds. Today this same area is called Antakya, Turkey, and in this modern metropolis, there is an archaeological museum that features the reconstruction of a very large home that once stood proudly in the nearby city of Daphne.

When the apostle Paul was sent out from Antioch to begin his apostolic ministry, he and his team members would have passed through Daphne and seen this home and many others like it. You can just imagine all the families who lived in these exquisite homes. There were moms and dads, grandmas and grandpas, children and grandchildren all living together, learning how to get along with each other.

Clearly, parents in that day needed solid biblical wisdom to raise good, godly children, and that is what Paul gave them. Today more than 2,000 years later, the same godly wisdom the Holy Spirit penned through him is still helping parents like you to shape and mold their children into strong, god-fearing adults.

The emphasis of this lesson:

Teaching your children to repent is teaching them to make a decision to agree with God and to change their behavior to line up with His standard of what *He* calls right according to His Word.

Repentance Is Foundational to Our Relationship With God

In our first lesson, we learned that the most important thing you can teach your children is to love Jesus above all else. Another vital truth they need to be taught is the practice of *repentance*. The word "repent" means *to make a decision to do something different. It is a change of one's heart and mind — a decision to turn away from sin and toward God. It is a decision to leave something behind and to change one's behavior.*

The principle of repentance is foundational and is seen throughout God's Word.

- The ministry of John the Baptist — the man who was sent by God to prepare the way for Jesus — was based entirely on repentance (*see* Luke 3:2-4).

- Jesus Himself began His ministry declaring, "...Repent: for the kingdom of heaven is at hand" (Matthew 4:17).

- The apostle Peter helped launch the Church on the day of Pentecost by saying, "...Repent, and be baptized..." (Acts 2:38).

- When the apostle Paul gave his infamous message to the learned men of Athens on Mars Hill, he declared that God "...commandeth all men every where to repent" (Acts 17:30).

- When Jesus spoke to the seven churches in the book of Revelation, again and again, He said, "Repent."

As you can see, the word "repent" is an important biblical term, and it is central to the Christian life. We enter the Kingdom of God through repentance, and it sets the course for the rest of our lives. We must understand it in order to be saved. Hence, we must teach our children the importance of repentance so that they might be saved, too, and live a life of peace in God's presence, blessing, and favor.

We Must Hear and Heed the Spirit's Voice

There are many people today who have mistakenly confused repentance with simply admitting wrong or asking for forgiveness for a wrong that they've done. While admitting wrong and asking for forgiveness is a *part* of repentance, there is more to it. *True repentance is a decision of one's will to change one's behavior.*

The Bible says, "A wise son heareth his father's instruction: but a scorner heareth not rebuke" (Proverbs 13:1). *Instructions* are usually given in calm, quiet voice tones. A *rebuke*, on the other hand, is usually spoken loudly, harshly, and hastily. A wise son or daughter is one that hears instruction and obeys; a scorner is one who turns a deaf ear to instruction and even refuses to listen to a rebuke that is yelled loudly.

When the Holy Spirit first begins to deal with us about something, He speaks instruction to us quietly. He is the still small voice inside us that is directing us and giving us time to repent and self-correct. If we don't repent, His voice grows louder and louder. His aim is to spare us from the pain of making wrong choices. If we refuse to hear and heed His instruction or rebuke — and *repent* — we will suffer the consequences of our wrong behavior.

What Does Teaching Repentance to Your Children Actually Look Like?

When your children do something wrong — when they blatantly disobey your instructions, act disrespectfully, treat their siblings wrongly, or have a bad attitude — they need to be taught to *repent*. For instance, if your son purposely did something you told him not to do, he needs to be told, "Son, you did exactly what I told you not to do. That is rebellion, and you need to *repent*. You need to admit what you did wrong, ask God and *us*, your parents, to forgive you — and make a decision to change your behavior."

To ensure your child knows what he or she did wrong, it is a good practice to ask that child, "What did you do that was wrong?" By doing this, you are helping your children recognize and take responsibility for their own actions. This practice is part of the repentance process they need to develop and understand, as it will stay with them throughout their lifetime.

It is important to understand that tears do not necessarily mean one has repented. Many people have cried a river of tears, but their wrong behavior never changed. Sometimes children will weep and wail to show that they are sorry in hopes of avoiding discipline. Don't let your child's tears fool you or keep you from correcting them. Real heart change that produces a change of behavior is what you're after — not tears. We know someone has truly repented when his or her behavior improves.

Always Administer Correction in Love

Once your child has repented — once he has admitted what he has done wrong, asked for forgiveness, and made the decision to change his behavior — giving him the proper correction or discipline is the next step. Always correct and discipline your children *in love* and give them an appropriate punishment for their inappropriate behavior.

Many times, a fitting punishment for wrong conduct is time out from playing or the removal of a special toy or privilege. Other times, it is necessary to apply what the Bible calls "the rod of correction" (*see* Proverbs 22:15). If you feel your child's disobedience or disrespect warrants a spanking on their bottom, always administer it while you are *calm*. If your emotions are out of control, send your son or daughter to his or her room for a few minutes so you can calm down and regain your composure.

After the discipline is carried out, tell your child you love him and give him a hug. Praying a quick prayer over your children is also strongly encouraged. As you hold them in your arms, you can pray a simple prayer like, "Father, thank You for [*your child's name*]. I pray You will help him [or her] change and begin doing what is right. Let [*your child's name*] know in his [or her] heart that You love him [or her] and want the very best for him [or her]. In Jesus' name, amen."

Repentance Opens the Door to God's Blessing

Teaching your children to repent is teaching them to make a decision to change their behavior. It is helping them realize that when they do wrong, they are to admit it, ask God for forgiveness, and ask anyone else they've hurt for forgiveness. Then they are to do whatever they need to do to change their behavior.

Keep in mind that repentance is a process that takes time. There isn't always an immediate transformation. In fact, the change in behavior you're seeking often occurs incrementally. This goes for adults and for children. But if your children continue to repent again and again and again, you will begin to see right behavior.

Essentially, repentance is agreeing with God — it is yielding to and submitting to His Spirit living inside us. And when we agree with the Holy Spirit, we open the door of blessing for Him to come and begin working in our lives and our situations.

By teaching repentance to your children, you are acknowledging that there is absolute truth. God has a higher standard — a standard of righteousness and holiness — that He calls us to live by (*see* 1 Peter 1:14-16; Leviticus 20:7,8). When your children repent, it positions them to walk in and experience God's very best. As they grow and mature, the Holy Spirit will continue to unpack the full measure of what repentance brings to their lives.

Things To Keep in Mind as You Teach Repentance

Demonstrate repentance. The best way to teach your children how to repent is to repent in front of them when you miss it and sin. For example, if you had a bad attitude and were harsh toward them, *repent.* Say, "I'm sorry for my irritable attitude toward you all. It was wrong for me to act that way. Please forgive me. I repent." Likewise, if you were impatient with your children, *repent.* Say, "Guys, I'm sorry for being impatient with you. I was wrong. God is extremely patient with me, and I need and want to be patient with you. Please forgive me. I repent."

There is no better way to teach right behavior than to demonstrate it before your children. Good, godly behavior will be *caught* by your example better than *taught* by your words. If you are going to require your children to repent, you need to show them how it's done. When your children see you humble yourself and have a willingness to acknowledge you were wrong and repent, you build a platform for them to be able to say, "Wow! If Dad and Mom can admit they were wrong and repent, I can do it too."

Call wrong behavior what God calls it — sin. As your children grow and are able to comprehend more, let them know that the wrong they have committed is *sin.* If they lie, cheat, steal, or hit their siblings, it is not a "mistake." It is *sin.* Explain to them how their sin hurts their relationship not only with you, but also with God. Tell them, "God loves you and He has great things prepared for you. But to experience the wonderful things He has planned, you need to obey Him and love Him with all your heart, soul, and strength."

Be consistent. As a parent, this is one of the most important things you can do for your children. As you train your kids in the way they should go — as you discipline them and require them to repent and ask for forgiveness — you need to be consistent. This means the standard of right and wrong remains the same. The behavior that is wrong on Monday is also wrong on Friday and Saturday. How you feel as a parent cannot affect the standard of right and wrong, nor can it determine whether or not you bring correction. Repentance is always required for wrong attitudes and actions, and correction must be meted when godly standards are violated. Consistency is a major key to seeing positive change.

Remember your job is temporary. It's important to remember that your children will not always live under your roof. The fact is, they will spend much more time living on their own than with you. As a parent, you are literally working yourself out of a job. The place of authority you hold in each of your children's lives is temporary. From birth onward, you are preparing them for a lifelong relationship with their heavenly Father. One day they will answer directly to Him, and He Himself will be correcting them and calling them to repent for wrong behavior.

STUDY QUESTIONS

> **Study to shew thyself approved unto God, a workman that needeth not to be ashamed, rightly dividing the word of truth.**
> — 2 Timothy 2:15

1. According to Acts 3:19 and Isaiah 55:7, what blessings come with our repentance?

2. When you correct your children, how would you describe your demeanor? Would you say you are calm and in control or angry, enraged, and out of control?

3. What does God say in James 1:19 and 20 about correcting your children to bring about right behavior? (Also consider Psalm 37:8; Ephesians 4:26,27.)

PRACTICAL APPLICATION

> **But be ye doers of the word, and not hearers only, deceiving your own selves.**
> — James 1:22

1. The best way to teach your children how to repent is to repent in front of them. Can you remember a time when you apologized to your kids for doing something wrong? What was their response to your willingness to repent? What changes did you notice in their behavior?

2. Are you willing to humble yourself before your children and admit when you're wrong? If not, why? Pray and ask the Holy Spirit to show you what is keeping you from demonstrating repentance.

3. Consistency as a parent, in things like your standard of right and wrong and bringing correction, is paramount to seeing positive change. On a scale of 1 to 5, how would you rate your consistency (1 being very inconsistent to 5 being very consistent)? In what areas do you need to come up higher? What is keeping you from being consistent that you need to remove from your life?

LESSON 3

TOPIC

Teach Your Children To Honor Authority

SCRIPTURES

1. **Ephesians 6:1-3** — Children, obey your parents in the Lord: for this is right. Honour thy father and mother; which is the first commandment with promise; That it may be well with thee, and thou mayest live long on the earth.

SYNOPSIS

The ancient city of Antioch was the third largest city in the Roman Empire. It was the place where the followers of Jesus Christ were first called Christians. It was also the town from which the apostle Paul and his assistant Barnabas launched out into full-time ministry. After the Holy Spirit said, "...Separate me Barnabas and Saul for the work whereunto I have called them" (Acts 13:2), Paul began his first missionary journey, heading down to the Mediterranean city of Seleucia.

Along the way, they passed through a town called Daphne, which was very wealthy and filled with many large homes. It was in these homes that husbands and wives, parents and grandparents, children and grandchildren lived and learned how to get along. The moms and dads who wanted to know how to raise up their children to be good, God-honoring adults received great wisdom from Paul — including his instructions on honoring authority.

The emphasis of this lesson:

Teaching your children to respect and honor authority is a must for them to enjoy a long and blessed life.

You Are the First Authority Your Kids Are To Honor and Respect

As we have noted, children do not automatically grow up into godly adults. On the contrary, the Bible says, "…They go astray as soon as they are born, speaking lies" (Psalm 58:3). Like a baby fish that innately knows how to swim from birth, children innately know how to sin. No one has to teach them how to lie, be selfish, or act rebelliously. At the very earliest age, the resident seeds of disobedience and disrespect effortlessly begin to sprout and will continue to produce nasty fruit unless we uproot it from their lives.

Therefore, in order for your children to honor and respect you as their parent, as well as honor and respect all those in positions of authority, you're going to have to *teach* them. In Ephesians 6:1-3 (*NKJV*), the apostle Paul spoke directly to children, saying, "Children, obey your parents in the Lord, for this is right. 'Honor your father and mother,' which is the first commandment with promise: 'that it may be well with you and you may live long on the earth.'"

As a parent — or a grandparent that is raising your grandchild — you are the first person of authority in your child's life. Thus, teaching them to honor and respect authority begins with teaching them how to honor and respect *you*. This character trait is essential for your kids to grow up and be prosperous and successful. If your children don't respect you, they will not respect anyone else in authority — including God. Disrespect and dishonor will only yield the unproductive fruit of death, not life, in their lives.

The Results of Careless Parenting Are Catastrophic

There are many parents today who are too lenient with their kids. They haven't taken the time to establish clear boundaries of right and wrong, and they don't require their kids to respect them or anyone else in authority. For many, the reason for this negligence is they just don't want to deal with the painful, laborious task of teaching and disciplining their children. Unfortunately, the pain and turmoil that result from their casual parenting is far worse.

If you look carefully at the lives of individuals who get into trouble, in most cases, they consistently disrespected and dishonored the people in authority in their lives. From the teachers and coaches who instructed them in school — to the managers and employers they worked for — to the law officers and government officials overseeing their city and state, they resisted and rebelled again and again.

People who don't pay their taxes, ignore traffic rules, and attempt to circumvent the law every chance they get usually live their lives going from one problem to another problem. Ironically, these same people are often quick to blame everyone else for the troubles in their life. Yet the common denominator in every situation is them. They refuse to submit to authority.

Honor and respect for authority is central to the health and survival of a family, a business, a church, and society. Imagine a family without parents, a church without a pastor, a country without a leader. The absence of respect and honor produces *chaos* and *anarchy*. Everyone becomes a law unto himself. This is one of the reasons we're dealing with such lawlessness in the world today. Therefore, when you look at your children, realize that you are not raising them to remain children. You are raising them to be *adults* — God-fearing, God-honoring adults who honor and respect authority.

Simple Yet Profound Ways To Cultivate Respect for Authority

It is so rare in our day and age to find people who understand and have respect for authority — especially young people. Young people who understand this principle and act on it are like precious jewels shining brightly in today's dark world. This is how your children appear in public when they are respectful and honoring. Some of the simplest, yet most important ways to establish a sense of honor and respect for authority in your kids as they grow is to require them to:

- Look you in the eyes when you are talking to them.
- Give you their undivided attention when you are speaking, as opposed to looking at television, their phone, a tablet, a computer, or any other distracting device.

- Answer, "Yes, ma'am," and, "Yes, sir" to you and to those in authority.
- Listen and not interrupt you (or those in authority) while you are speaking.
- Refrain from verbally cutting down their teachers, coaches, relatives, and government officials.

Although some of their responses and interruptions may seem cute when they are little, those responses quickly turn into disrespect that must be corrected. As you choose to raise your children to honor and respect those in authority, you are preparing them to live a blessed, long life.

Remember To Monitor Your Children's Media Choices

It is wonderful to see how much effort and care that so many parents are putting into their children's daily diet these days. With the growing problems of obesity and other health risks among children, we do need to be mindful of what our kids are eating. Likewise, it is just as important for us to be mindful of what is on your children's *media* menu.

Much of today's music, television, and movies are saturated with dishonoring and disrespectful speech. One cutting remark is quickly followed by another with a splash of profanity mixed in here and there. The emasculation of men and the degradation of women are unabashedly on display, and beneath much of the dialogue is an enhanced laugh track that has been cleverly laid. Even some of the not-so-new movies and sitcoms are spiked with the same kind of content.

That said, you need to be mindful of what your child is feeding his or her soul and spirit. The psalmist David said in 101:3, "I will set not wicked thing before mine eyes...." What your children *behold* with their eyes and hear with their ears, they will become. So make every effort to present them with age-appropriate, healthy media alternatives. There are a number of quality media choices available, including music, movies, and shows that honor God and help instill His Word in your child's heart.

'What Am I To Teach My Kids About Honoring Corrupt Authority?'

History reveals that believers living in early New Testament times experienced much injustice and persecution for their faith. Many lost their jobs, had their possessions confiscated, and were physically abused, tortured, and even killed. Yet not once were they told to rebel against authority. On the contrary, they were instructed to *honor*, *respect*, and *submit to* their rulers — even Nero, one of the most wicked rulers who ever lived.

The Bible says, "Let every soul be subject to the governing authorities. For there is no authority except from God, and the authorities that exist are appointed by God. Therefore, whoever resists the authority resists the ordinance of God, and those who resist will bring judgment on themselves" (Romans 13:1,2 *NKJV*).

The truth is, even if the authority over you is unjust, it doesn't give you the right to disrespect them. If you are in the right and you honor them, you will outlast them. The same is true for your children. If they're being unjustly treated by their teacher, principal, or coach, teach them to bring their hurt to God and not verbalize it to everyone else. As they maintain a respectful attitude, God will change them in the process and bring them out of the situation better than ever.

If you really want to give the devil a black eye, take your child by the hand and begin to pray for their unjust leaders with them. Whenever you pray for any leader — your pastor, president, teacher, governor, or grandparents — it greatly pleases God (*see* 1 Timothy 2:1-3), and it is a wonderful way to teach your children how to honor and respect authority.

Yes, teaching your children to honor authority is tedious. It requires tireless effort for you to give the same instruction and the same correction again and again and again. But the rewards far outweigh the work. By doing so, you are positioning your kids to live a long, happy, productive life!

STUDY QUESTIONS

Study to shew thyself approved unto God, a workman that needeth not to be ashamed, rightly dividing the word of truth.
— 2 Timothy 2:15

1. The Bible has much to say about authority and how we are to treat them. Take a few moments to reflect on Exodus 22:28; Ecclesiastes 10:20; First Peter 2:17; and Romans 13:1 and 2. In your own words, what is the Holy Spirit speaking to you about how you treat

authority? Is there anything He is showing you about your attitude or actions of which you need to repent? If so, what is it?

2. One of the best ways to teach your children to honor those in authority is *to pray for their leaders with them.* Read them God's directive in First Timothy 2:1-4 and explain why He wants us to pray for those in authority over us.

PRACTICAL APPLICATION

> But be ye doers of the word, and not hearers only,
> deceiving your own selves.
> —James 1:22

1. What you model in front of your children instructs them and has a greater impact on their lives than what you say. Be honest. How would you describe *your* attitude toward the people in authority in your life? What types of comments come out of your mouth regarding people like your pastor, the president, government officials, and police officers? Would you feel good about seeing your attitude and actions toward authority duplicated in your kids? If not, what do you need to do to change the direction in which you're going?

2. It's important for you to know what's on your children's media menu. Take some time to learn about and make a quick list of the TV shows and movies they are watching, the type of music they're listening to, and the video games they're playing. Are there any media options you need to delete? What might be some healthier media alternatives for them? (Consider checking out PluggedIn.com; RightNowMedia.com as well as PureFlix.com for other options.)

LESSON 4

TOPIC

Teach Your Children To Work

SCRIPTURES

1. **2 Thessalonians 3:10** — For even when we were with you, this we commanded you, that if any would not work, neither should he eat.

SYNOPSIS

Memories of a "home life gone by" are a major component of archaeological museums in Antakya, Turkey. In this modern-day metropolis, known in early New Testament times as the city of Antioch, is a phenomenal collection of mosaics, which are like modern-day carpets that have been excavated from homes that once stood throughout the region. There is also a reconstruction of a very large Roman house from the Second Century. When one views these amazing artifacts, it's not hard to imagine children playing on the floors of these homes, moms and grandmothers working together in the kitchen to prepare family meals, and fathers and grandfathers laboring to earn an income to provide for the family's needs.

As a parent, your role is vital in the lives of your children. There are many things educators and other professionals can teach them, but there are some things that only you as a mother or father can teach and instill in them. Thus far, we have seen that we need to teach our children — and grandchildren — three very important things: First and foremost, *to love Jesus above all else*; second, the practice of *repentance*; and third, *to honor and respect authority*. The fourth essential life lesson they need to learn from us is *how to develop a good work ethic*.

The emphasis of this lesson:

Teaching your children how to work with excellence and professionalism in everything they do is vital to their success.

God is a God of excellence, and everything He does is first-class. And He instructs us as His children to imitate Him (*see* Ephesians 5:1). Therefore, since He is actively working in the world, we, too, are to be at work. Ecclesiastes 9:10 (*NIV*) says, "Whatever your hand finds to do, do it with all your might…." And in Colossians 3:23 (*NIV*), this instruction is reiterated through Paul who said, "Whatever you do, work at it with all your heart, as working for the Lord, not for men."

Although our society tends to teach an entitlement mentality, the reality is that work is an inseparable part of life. Anything worthwhile takes effort and hard work. In fact, work is so important that the Bible says, "…If any would not work, neither should he eat" (2 Thessalonians 3:10). Therefore, in order to share in the harvest, we must do our share of the work.

Opportunities To Work Abound
All Around Your Home

It is your responsibility as a parent to pass on a good work ethic to your sons and daughters from the very earliest of ages. One of the first things you can teach them to do is pick up after themselves, which includes cleaning their room. Other early learning opportunities include emptying the trash, cleaning up after the dog, and clearing the table. Jobs like these are great for kids to learn how to follow instructions and to develop discipline.

If you think about it, the kinds of job opportunities around your house are many and varied. Children can learn a good work ethic by sweeping the floor, dusting the furniture, vacuuming the carpet, washing dishes, folding their clothes, or mowing the lawn. No task is too small. It is actually quite amazing to watch even the smallest of toddlers begin to help around the house with just a little praise and encouragement.

With every task your children complete, character is forged within them. They learn to take responsibility, maintain a good attitude, and do what it takes to get the job done. Loyalty, reliability, and a sense of ownership are also instilled. Qualities like these are priceless and will stay with them throughout their adult years.

A Good Work Ethic Develops Diligence

In our first lesson, we looked at Proverbs 22:6, which says, "Train up a child in the way he should go: and when he is old, he will not depart from it." We saw that the word "train" in Hebrew is connected with the development of one's *taste buds*. Specifically, it depicts parents who start their children out early eating healthy foods. When those children are fully-grown, they will return to eating those same nutritious foods they developed an appetite for when they were little.

Similarly, we saw that when you train up your children to love Jesus — giving them a healthy appetite for the things of God when they are little — when they are older, they won't depart from it. And the same principle applies to developing a good work ethic. If you train up your children to enjoy the taste of working hard and experiencing the satisfaction of a job well done, they will develop a healthy appetite for work and keep coming back for more.

The Bible says, "Lazy hands make a man poor, but diligent hands bring wealth" (Proverbs 10:4 *NIV*). Indeed, "The sluggard craves and gets nothing, but the desires of the diligent are fully satisfied" (Proverbs 13:4 *NIV*). The diligent are the hardworking and industrious — those who take their responsibilities seriously. By training up your children to have a good work ethic, you instill diligence within them and set them up for success. As Proverbs 14:23 (*MSG*) says, "Hard work always pays off...."

Include Your Kids in the Work You're Doing

Rick and Denise Renner included their sons in the work of the ministry when their children were very young. From folding and stuffing thousands of envelopes at the office to setting up and tearing down the equipment for weekly services, they learned to see that what they did was very important. Cutting the grass, raking leaves, and removing snow from the sidewalks were not just about filling time. These were vital assignments that allowed the ministry of spreading the Gospel to continue.

Rick and Denise placed a high value on every task, which enabled their sons to see their contribution as significant. They learned that every job they did was done unto God (*see* Colossians 3:23), and they considered it a privilege and an honor to be a part of it. The more involved they became, the more valuable their input grew, and the more they learned and developed as workers and servants of God.

What part of your work can you invite your children to do with you? Although you may not be able to take them to your office, there may be some aspects of your work in which you can include them. Maybe there are some tasks around the house that you can delegate to them in which they can take personal ownership. It's true that they won't do things exactly the way you would, and they may even make mistakes as they start out. But everyone has to begin somewhere. God gives you a chance to grow and make mistakes, and you should extend the same kind of grace to your kids. Giving them opportunities to work will impact them in ways you could never imagine.

Remember, your children learn just as much, if not more, by your example of hard work than by what you *say* about the importance of hard work. By observing your diligence and excellence in action, they will learn what to do and what not to do. An exceptional life is a result of exceptional effort. So don't complain about your job or the people with whom you work.

Being able to work is a privilege — just ask someone who is unemployed and looking for a job. As you take every moment you are given to teach your children, your grandchildren, your nieces, and your nephews the rich rewards of consistent hard work, you will successfully pass along the gift of a good work ethic to the next generation.

STUDY QUESTIONS

Study to shew thyself approved unto God, a workman that needeth not to be ashamed, rightly dividing the word of truth.
— 2 Timothy 2:15

1. What does Proverbs 22:29 say will happen to your children as they become skilled and diligent in their work?

2. The Bible calls hard work *diligence*. According to these passages in the book of Proverbs, what blessings can your children expect for developing diligence? What curses produced by *laziness* (slothfulness) do they need to avoid? (*See* Proverbs 10:4; 12:24; 13:4; 15:19; 21:5, 25; 24:30-34).

The *blessings* of diligence: _____

_____

The *curses* of laziness: _____

_____

PRACTICAL APPLICATION

But be ye doers of the word, and not hearers only, deceiving your own selves.
—James 1:22

1. Who would you say served as a role model of hard-work in your life? What do you remember most about how they worked? What did their example and words of instruction instill in you that you are still using to this day?

2. What part of your work can you invite your children to do with you? Are there any meetings they could attend with you? If you cannot take them to your office, are there any assignments in which you can include them? What special tasks around the house can you delegate to them and allow them to take personal ownership of?

3. The way your children perform their household tasks will greatly determine the quality of their worth ethic as adults. In what practical ways can you help them cultivate a work ethic of excellence as they carry out their chores?

LESSON 5

TOPIC

Teach Your Children To Value Material Possessions and To Be Thankful

SCRIPTURES

1. **Proverbs 12:27** — The slothful man roasteth not that which he took in hunting: but the substance of a diligent man is precious.

SYNOPSIS

The ancient city of Antioch — the place where believers were first called Christians — was a large, wealthy city sprawling with many beautiful homes and villas. We've noted in previous lessons that the archaeological museum in Antakya, Turkey, which was constructed on the ruins of ancient Antioch, has a collection of mosaics from these homes that were excavated from around the region. Families lived in these houses — families just like yours — with parents who were doing their best to train up and raise good children.

Thus far, we have examined four specific things you as a parent need to teach your children and the children God placed in your life. The first attribute is *to love Jesus above all else*. More than anything else you can teach, this is paramount. The second thing you need to teach them is *to repent* — to not only admit when they're wrong and to ask for forgiveness, but also to make a decision to change their behavior. The third life lesson is *to honor and respect authority*, and the fourth is *to work*. The Bible says that if a man doesn't work, he should not eat (*see* 2 Thessalonians 3:10). These things are all foundational to your kids building a healthy life.

The emphasis of this lesson:

Teaching your children to value money and material possessions — and to be thankful —are two more very important qualities your kids need to cultivate in order to be successful, godly adults.

The Difference Between the Lazy and the Diligent

Teaching your children to value money and material possessions is important, as it fosters a sincere appreciation for what they have and fights against a lazy, uncaring attitude. Proverbs 12:27 says, "The slothful man roasteth not that which he took in hunting: but the substance of a diligent man is precious." In this verse, the word "slothful" means *lazy*. Thus, this scripture tells us that the lazy man is like a person who catches and kills an animal for food, but then does nothing with it. He is so irresponsible with and unthankful for what he has that he carelessly leaves the animal to rot.

The diligent man, on the other hand, is *a hard-working* man. He is thankful and responsible, and to him, *all* his substance, which is every-thing he has, is precious. There is great appreciation that flows from one who is diligent and has been taught a good work ethic. He recognizes the importance of valuing money and material possessions and makes good use of all that he has.

Years ago, we didn't have the abundance of goods we have today, nor did we have easy access to virtually anything at the touch of a finger. In those days, children who received a new set of clothes and shoes at Easter or at the start of a new school year were extremely grateful. Even hand-me-downs were a welcomed sight to a child who had outgrown his clothes. In many ways, having less was having more. Parents and children had a greater appreciation for material goods, home-cooked meals, and a few extra dollars in their pockets. People were more diligent, and all their substance was precious to them.

Today, nearly everyone lives with an abundant supply and instant access to just about anything they desire via high-speed Internet and computers and phones. Unfortunately, many people think having plenty is normal, and amidst this setting of abundance, a growing sense of ungratefulness and dissatisfaction has emerged. Society at large — especially children — feel entitled to everything. "Entitlement" is an unspoken belief that one has a right to and deserves something.

There is nothing inherently wrong with having abundance, and there is nothing wrong with teaching your kids to believe God for more. God is a generous God, and Jesus came to give us life and life more abundant (*see* John 10:10). The real problem is the attitude of *unthankfulness* and a *lack of appreciation* that often accompanies abundance. So as you teach you kids to believe for more, also teach them to recognize and appreciate all that they already have. And when God blesses them with more than they need or can contain, encourage them to look around for someone in need they can give to and show the love of God.

Be Generous *and* Wise With Your Children

Thankfully, God in His infinite wisdom doesn't give us everything we ask for *all at once*. The first and most obvious reason is because we couldn't handle it. Second, we most likely wouldn't appreciate it. And third, we would probably waste most of it because we wouldn't be able to manage it all.

The way God deals with us is the way we should deal with our children. Yes, we should be generous, but we also need to be very wise. For the reasons just mentioned, we should not give them everything they ask for all at once. Instead, we need to prayerfully and carefully give to our children and teach them to value and appreciate money and material possessions.

How are they caring for the possessions you've already given them? For instance, do they leave their nice, new clothes strewn out on the floor or do they put them away? How about the bike they wanted so desperately? Or the latest and greatest video game system you gave them for Christmas? And what have they done with the money you gave them the last time they asked for it? If they take care of what you've given them and are thankful for it, then they are ready to receive more.

If you think about it, money is a form of power, and it is a test in the hands of those who have it. What you do with the money you have determines whether you are worthy of greater responsibility and power — spiritual power. When people don't understand money, they usually don't value it, and they become wasteful. As a result of their squandering, they disqualify themselves from receiving greater income and greater power. This is an important truth you need to teach your children.

So before you buy them something else or hand them another fist full of dollars, you need to stop and ask yourself — and the Holy Spirit — some pointed questions: *Do they really need this? If so, why do they need it? Are they taking care of the possessions I've already given them? Have they wisely invested the money I gave them last time, or have they squandered it on worthless things?* The answers to these questions reveal what actions you should take.

Choosing To Be Thankful Is Powerful!

Another very valuable lesson to teach your children is *to be thankful.* Through the apostle Paul, the Holy Spirit said, "In every thing give thanks: for this is the will of God in Christ Jesus concerning you" (1 Thessalonians 5:18). When you and your children choose to be thankful, you change your atmosphere and the direction in which you are heading.

The truth is, we cannot complain and be thankful at the same time. We can only do one or the other. If you choose complaining, your demeanor will sink into sadness, despair, and bitterness. But if you choose to be thankful, your disposition will rise to experience peace, joy, and hope. It's no wonder Paul instructed us to, "Do all things without grumbling and faultfinding and complaining [against God] and questioning and doubting [among yourselves]" (Philippians 2:14 *AMPC*). Without question, a *thankful* heart is truly a *happy* heart!

It is interesting to note that the Holy Spirit prophesied through Paul in Second Timothy 3:1 and 2 that in the last of the last days, there would be a widespread epidemic of unthankful people. Many signs today confirm that we are presently living in these predicted times. Ironically, even though the majority of people are living in abundance and have access to virtually everything they could ever want, they are more ungrateful and dissatisfied than ever.

The fact is, unthankful people live miserable lives. They are never happy or satisfied with anything. Instead, they murmur and complain about everything. The Corinthian believers had become haughty, thinking more highly of themselves than they should. To address their pride, Paul asked them, "...What do you have that you did not receive? And if you did receive it, why do you boast as if you had not received it?" (1 Corinthians 4:7 *NASB*.) If you take time to stop and honestly think about it, you will see how true and spot-on James 1:17 is: "Every good gift and every perfect gift is from above, and cometh down from the Father...."

The truth is, there are countless things for which you and your children can be thankful. Think about it. If you're breathing, that is something for which to be thankful! If you're all at home and not in a hospital or prison, that is a reason to be thankful. If you have food in your fridge and pantry and a vehicle to get you around, those are all things for which to be thankful. How about salvation? Has Jesus Christ saved you from eternal punishment in hell and cleansed you of all your sin? Friend, that is a reason to be thankful and eternally thrilled!

Where there is thankfulness, the atmosphere it charged with the presence of God. Psalm 100:4 (*AMPC*) says, "Enter into His gates with thanksgiving and a thank offering and into His courts with praise! Be thankful and say so to Him, bless and affectionately praise His name!"

Please realize if you don't teach your children to be thankful and express their thanks with words, they will naturally be unthankful. So teach your children to be thankful and to say "thank you" all the time. Teach them to say, "Thank You" to God daily for every wonderful blessing He has given them — big or small. Thank Him for every meal they eat, every sunrise they see, and every other blessing He brings their way. Tell them to say "thank you" to their teachers for teaching them and to the public servants — like firemen, policemen, and military personnel — who protect them.

Remember, your children learn just as much, if not more, from your example than by what you say. So lead the way in being thankful. If you have had a tendency to murmur and complain, repent. Ask God to forgive you, receive His forgiveness, and make a decision to change. Another powerful thing you can do is to apologize to your children for being negative. Then pray together, asking God to change your perspectives and to enable you to see all the good things for which you can all be thankful. Indeed, "How good it is to give thanks to you, O Lord, to sing in your honor, O Most High God" (Psalm 92:1 *GNT*).

STUDY QUESTIONS

Study to shew thyself approved unto God, a workman that needeth not to be ashamed, rightly dividing the word of truth.
— 2 Timothy 2:15

1. Have you had a tendency to murmur and complain? If so, how has it affected your thinking and the atmosphere of your life? What effects has it had on your children?

2. Again and again, God's Word instructs us to "give thanks" and "be thankful." The apostle Paul gave thanks repeatedly, and the psalmist admonished us to give thanks in dozens of verses. What rewarding fruit have you experienced from being thankful?

3. The Bible says, "Godliness with contentment is great gain" (1 Timothy 6:6). How can you cultivate a heart of contentment? Carefully reflect on God's words through Paul in First Timothy 6:6-11 along with the wisdom of Proverbs 15:16 and Hebrews 13:5.

PRACTICAL APPLICATION

But be ye doers of the word, and not hearers only,
deceiving your own selves.
—James 1:22

As we complete our final lesson, stop and take a personal inventory of how you are doing in the areas we have covered. Ask yourself these questions and answer as honestly as you can.

1. *How am I doing with teaching my children to love Jesus above all else?*

2. *How am I doing with teaching my children to repent?*

3. *How am I doing with teaching my children to honor and respect authority?*

4. *How am I doing with teaching my children to work?*

5. *How am I doing with teaching my children to value money and material possessions and to be thankful?*

In light of your answers, where do you need the most help from the Holy Spirit? Is there anything you need to repent of? If God is dealing with you about something, know that He is *not* mad at you. He loves you dearly and wants the very best for you and your children. Take some time to pour your heart out to Him and invite Him into your life and your children's lives. He will give you the grace to be the best parent you can possibly be and to teach your children what they need to learn to ensure a good life!

A Prayer To Receive Salvation

If you've never received Jesus as your Savior and Lord, now is the time for you to experience the new life Jesus wants to give you! To receive God's gift of salvation that can be obtained through Jesus alone, pray this prayer from your heart:

Jesus, I repent of my sin and receive You as my Savior and Lord. Wash away my sin with Your precious blood and make me completely new. I thank You that my sin is removed, and Satan no longer has any right to lay claim on me. Through Your empowering grace, I faithfully promise that I will serve You as my Lord for the rest of my life.

If you just prayed this prayer of salvation, you are born again! You are a brand-new creation in Christ! Would you please let us know of your decision by going to **renner.org/salvation**? We would love to connect with you and pray for you as you begin your new life in Christ.

Scriptures for further study: John 3:16; John 14:6; Acts 4:12; Ephesians 1:7; Hebrews 10:19,20; 1 Peter 1:18,19; Romans 10:9,10; Colossians 1:13; 2 Corinthians 5:17; Romans 6:4; 1 Peter 1:3

Notes

Notes

_____

_____

_____

_____

_____

_____

_____

_____

_____

_____

_____

_____

_____

_____

_____

_____

_____

_____

_____

_____

_____

_____

_____

_____

CLAIM YOUR FREE RESOURCE!

As a way of introducing you further to the teaching ministry of Rick Renner, we would like to send you FREE of charge his teaching, "How To Receive a Miraculous Touch From God" on CD or as an MP3 download.

In His earthly ministry, Jesus commonly healed *all* who were sick of *all* their diseases. In this profound message, learn about the manifold dimensions of Christ's wisdom, goodness, power, and love toward all humanity who came to Him in faith with their needs.

☑ **YES, I want to receive Rick Renner's monthly teaching letter!**

Simply scan the QR code to claim this resource or go to: **renner.org/claim-your-free-offer**

Connect WITH US!

R renner.org

f facebook.com/rickrenner • facebook.com/rennerdenise

▶ youtube.com/rennerministries • youtube.com/deniserenner

○ instagram.com/rickrenner • instagram.com/rennerministries_
instagram.com/rennerdenise

www.ingramcontent.com/pod-product-compliance
Lightning Source LLC
Chambersburg PA
CBHW070757050426
42452CB00010B/1869